Deborah: Prophetess and Warrior

Deborah: Prophetess and Warrior

A New Commentary
by Gene Allen Groner

To

_____

From

_____

Other Books by Gene Allen Groner

Available in paperback and Kindle eBooks

Journey of a Disciple

The Garden of Eden

Native American Prayers Poems and Legends

Native American Horses

Native American Fine Art

Micah's Fine Art

Fine Art by Sassan Filsoof

Son of the Most High

-These Three Remain

The Helper: a Discourse on the Holy Spirit

Hallowed Be Thy Name

Deborah: Prophetess and Warrior

Saint Teresa of Calcutta

From Shepherd to King: the Story of David

The Nature of Angels

Speak To This People: Bible Prophets and Prophecies

For Such a Time as This: the Story of Esther

Prayers and Poems of Christ

In the Beginning

Take Off Your Sandals: the story of Moses

The Silver-Tongued Prophet: the Story of Isaiah

My God is Yahweh: the Story of Elijah

Meditations

Evangelist Billy Graham

World's Greatest Missionary: the Apostle Paul

2020 Poems

Stairway to Heaven

Full of Grace

Jesus' Hands Are Kind Hands

The Kingdom of Heaven

From Genesis to Revelation: Women in the Bible

Testify

Revelation

The Cross

Introduction

Deborah: Prophetess and Warrior

The story of Deborah is intriguing. Gifted as a leader, military strategist, and seer Deborah stands out among the women of the Bible as a unique and faithful follower of the Lord. Follow her story as she forges a trail of mystery and victory through the pages of history.

Though we know little of her early years, we know her strength of character and unusual abilities. Follow her on her journey toward the destiny the Lord has prepared for her. See her in action. Listen to her voice as she speaks for the people of Israel, and she leads us on her wondrous adventure of life and legend.

The author includes his commentary on each section, dissecting the text and writing his own interpretation in italics at the end of the verses. New insights and thoughts are forthcoming in this interesting and valuable New Testament commentary on an Old Testament story. You will want to study and learn more from this fascinating woman of faith and courage.

Deborah: Prophetess and Warrior

A New Commentary
by Gene Allen Groner

Judges 4

Good News Translation (GNT)

Deborah and Barak

1 After Ehud died, the people of Israel sinned against the Lord again. 2 So the Lord let them be conquered by Jabin, a Canaanite king who ruled in the city of Hazor. The commander of his army was Sisera, who lived at Harosheth-of-the-Gentiles. 3 Jabin had nine hundred iron chariots, and he ruled the people of Israel with cruelty and violence for twenty years. Then the people of Israel cried out to the Lord for help.

The history of Israel repeats itself again. Over and over they fall in line and love the Lord above anything else, and then they fall out of love with God and fall in love with some other idol, usually Baal, the calf god of fertility. Why they behave this way is hard to say. Is it complacency, a fickle nature, allow themselves to fall into temptation and don't want to get out of the relationship? Or do they become discontented with their God and lose interest in doing the right things? Or maybe they follow whatever leader happens to be in power, be it judge or king. Whatever the reason, it takes a prophet (or in the case of Deborah) or a prophetess.

4 Now Deborah, the wife of Lappidoth, was a prophet, and she was serving as a judge for the Israelites at that time. 5 She would sit under a certain palm tree between Ramah and Bethel in the hill country of Ephraim, and the people of Israel would go there for her decisions.

A prophet and a judge. The role of a prophet in ancient Israel was first and foremost to be a representative of the Lord, Yahweh. The prophet represented the Lord in boldly stating the truth to those in power, regardless of the consequences. Dreams and visions often accompanied the spoken word, where the prophet would give the interpretation of dreams or visions on behalf of the Lord.

Depending on the circumstances, the prophet would advise, warn, reprimand, and guide and direct the leader in power. On occasion he or she would speak directly to the people of Israel regarding the direction they were heading or the behavior they were counseled to correct.

Praying was one of the tasks of the prophet, as when Elijah prayed for fire to demonstrate God's supremacy over Baal and the other gods, and then prayed for rain to provide water for crops and for drinking. When praying, the prophet never rested until the prayer was answered.

A key role of the prophet was in the area of worship, at times leading the worship for Israel, as when the sister of Moses led the worship of God after the Israelites crossed over the Sea.

As to the role of judge, during the time of the conquest of Canaan, it was the role of the judges to lead the people in the worship of the one true God, Yahweh, and to call them back to their covenant relationship with him.

When needed, which was much too frequently, the judges were called upon to save the Israelites from their enemies. In that position, it was not uncommon for the judges to take the role of warrior and leader of the armed forces. Such was the calling of the Judge Deborah, as we shall soon see.

6 One day she sent for Barak son of Abinoam from the city of Kedesh in Naphtali and said to him, "The Lord, the God of Israel, has given you this command: 'Take ten thousand men from the tribes of Naphtali and Zebulun and lead them to Mount Tabor. 7 I will bring Sisera, the commander of Jabin's army, to fight you at the Kishon River. He will have his chariots and soldiers, but I will give you victory over him.'"

8 Then Barak replied, "I will go if you go with me, but if you don't go with me, I won't go either."

9 She answered, "All right, I will go with you, but you won't get any credit for the victory, because the Lord will hand Sisera over to a woman." So Deborah set off for Kedesh with Barak. 10 Barak called the tribes of Zebulun and Naphtali to Kedesh, and ten thousand men followed him. Deborah went with him.

The name Abinoam means "divine father of pleasantness." The name probably suits his son Barak better, because although Barak is the military general, his demeanor and attitude are more like the "pleasantness" of his father—he didn't have the heart to lead the fight against Sisera and the army of Jabin at Mount Tabor. He wouldn't agree to go to battle until Deborah agreed to go with him, in effect "holding his hand."

I have known men like that—leaders in name only—who would shrink at the first sight of conflict.

Deborah, on the other hand, was a true leader, both on the field and off the field. She didn't hesitate to lead the troops against the commander of Jabin's army. She knew that her God would be there and win the battle for Israel. One is reminded of David the shepherd boy going up against the Philistine giant Goliath. There was no fear in her, just as there was no fear in David. They both knew who would be victorious. That's the sign of a great leader.

11 In the meantime Heber the Kenite had set up his tent close to Kedesh near the oak tree at Zaanannim. He had moved away from the other Kenites, the descendants of Hobab, the brother-in-law of Moses.

12 When Sisera learned that Barak had gone up to Mount Tabor, 13 he called out his nine hundred iron chariots and all his men, and sent them from Harosheth-of-the-Gentiles to the Kishon River.

14 Then Deborah said to Barak, "Go! The Lord is leading you! Today he has given you victory over Sisera." So Barak went down from Mount Tabor with his ten thousand men. 15 When Barak attacked with his army, the Lord threw Sisera into confusion together with all his chariots and men. Sisera got down from his chariot and fled on foot. 16 Barak pursued the chariots and the army to Harosheth-of-the-Gentiles, and Sisera's whole army was killed. Not a man was left.

God calls his followers to a life of courage, not cowardice, faith not fear, and when we move out if full faith in him we are assured the victory.

In the case of Barak, he moved forward not in faith, but in fear of the larger army with its chariots and seasoned fighting men. But the prophetess and warrior was the one who knew the victory belonged to God. She was the one who demonstrated the courage, not cowardice. And she is the one to whom God gave the credit.

There is an eternal principle here that we don't want to miss. It is the divine principle of honoring the God of our fathers, the God of Abraham, Isaac, and Jacob. The God of Moses and Aaron. The God of the Prophetess and Judge Deborah. Here is the principle: Honor God and he will honor you. No doubt. No fear. Only faith and trust in the one true God, the God of Israel. Honor God and God will honor you.

17 Sisera ran away to the tent of Jael, the wife of Heber the Kenite, because King Jabin of Hazor was at peace with Heber's family. 18 Jael went out to meet Sisera and said to him, "Come in, sir; come into my tent. Don't be afraid." So he went in, and she hid him behind a curtain. 19 He said to her, "Please give me a drink of water; I'm thirsty." She opened a leather bag of milk, gave him a drink, and hid him again. 20 Then he told her, "Stand at the door of the tent, and if anyone comes and asks you if anyone is here, say no."

21 Sisera was so tired that he fell sound asleep. Then Jael took a hammer and a tent peg, quietly went up to him, and killed him by driving the peg right through the side of his head and into the ground. 22 When Barak came looking for Sisera, Jael went out to meet him and said to him, "Come here! I'll show you the man you're looking for." So he went in with her, and there was Sisera on the ground, dead, with the tent peg through his head.

What we see here in the scripture passage is replayed over and over again in the history of Israel. Dishonor God and God will dishonor you—the second part of the divine eternal principle outlined in the previous comments I made. Sisera dishonored God, and God arranged to dishonor Sisera. Go up against the God of Israel and you will be dishonored—guaranteed.

23 That day God gave the Israelites victory over Jabin, the Canaanite king. 24 They pressed harder and harder against him until they destroyed him.

Judges 5

Good News Translation (GNT)

The Song of Deborah and Barak

On that day Deborah and Barak son of Abinoam sang this song:

Praise the Lord!

The Israelites were determined to fight;

the people gladly volunteered.

Listen, you kings!

Pay attention, you rulers!

I will sing and play music

to Israel's God, the Lord.

Lord, when you left the mountains of Seir,

when you came out of the region of Edom,

the earth shook, and rain fell from the sky.

Yes, water poured down from the clouds.

The mountains quaked before the Lord of
Sinai,

before the Lord, the God of Israel.

In the days of Shamgar son of Anath,

in the days of Jael,

caravans no longer went through the land,

and travelers used the back roads.

The towns of Israel stood abandoned,

Deborah;

they stood empty until you came,

came like a mother for Israel.

Then there was war in the land

when the Israelites chose new gods.

Of the forty thousand men in Israel,

did anyone carry shield or spear?

My heart is with the commanders of Israel,

with the people who gladly volunteered.

Praise the Lord!

Tell of it, you that ride on white donkeys,

sitting on saddles,

and you that must walk wherever you go

Listen! The noisy crowds around the well

are telling of the Lord's victories,

the victories of Israel's people!

Then the Lord's people marched down

from their cities.

Lead on, Deborah, lead on!

Lead on! Sing a song! Lead on!

Forward, Barak son of Abinoam,

lead your captives away!

The victory was God's victory, and the credit he gladly gave to Deborah. Barak was relegated to "leading the captives away."

There is a popular saying going around: "There is no limit to what you can accomplish if you don't care who gets the credit." Ronald Reagan is known to have had that engraved on a plaque on his desk in the Oval Office, but he didn't invent it. The saying was originally made by Ralph

Waldo Emerson, the 19th century American essayist, lecturer, and poet. Reagan was glad to take the credit for the saying, but the honor goes to Emerson, in my opinion.

So here we have another eternal principle: in everything you do, be humble about it and give God the credit. Let me put Emerson's saying this way:

"There is no limit to what you can accomplish, when you care enough to give the credit to God."

An old campfire song goes, "Rise and shine and give God the glory, glory. Rise and shine and give God the glory, glory. Rise and shine and give God the glory, glory...children of the Lord."

That's the best advice I can offer.

Then the faithful ones came down to their

leaders;

the Lord's people came to him ready to

fight.

They came from Ephraim into the valley,

behind the tribe of Benjamin and its

people.

The commanders came down from Machir,

 the officers down from Zebulun.

 The leaders of Issachar came with

Deborah;

 yes, Issachar came and Barak too,

 and they followed him into the valley.

Workers and warriors, they all respond in the same way. Show them a leader who is brave and visionary and they will follow them anywhere. The principle applies equally well on the battlefield, in the workplace, or in the church. Be a leader people want to follow, and they will. Show them what you're made of, and they'll show you what they are made of. Lead from the front like a real leader, and they will follow you wherever you lead them.

Jesus and his disciples knew this principle well. Jesus always led from the front, never from the rear. He was out front in his ministry of teaching and preaching and healing the sick. He was the visionary that the disciples readily followed, wherever he led them. They knew they could depend on

Jesus to take them places they would not normally go on their own. Jesus knew the way.

He said, "I am the way, the truth, and the light." And the disciples understood that Jesus meant what he said—he practiced what he preached. This was evident from the beginning, when he without hesitation asked his cousin John the Baptist to baptize him. When John hesitated, Jesus didn't. He said it had to be that way "in order to fulfill all righteousness." What he meant was this: He always did the will of the Father. He followed. Followed the lead of his Father in heaven.

This brings to light the next eternal principle I want to emphasize: A good leader knows how to follow orders. Repeat: A good leader knows how to follow orders. He knows that he can't expect you to follow his lead if he isn't willing to do the work himself. That is as true and applicable today as it was over 2000 years ago, as it was in the time of Adam and Eve. Truth is truth, regardless of the time it first appears. Truth is eternal—it exists in a sphere of its own. Truth comes from God himself. It is like God. It is the same yesterday, today, and tomorrow. Truth exists in a sphere of its own.

Truth is not relative—good for now in this situation, but not good tomorrow in a different situation. Truth is always true. God is always true. Jesus is always true. We can and should depend on it.

There is another thing about truth. Intelligence is light and truth. That is why Jesus is the most intelligent person ever created. When he said he is the "light and the truth" he was speaking from his intellect as well as his heart. God gave Jesus everything under his control, everything on earth was to be under his control. He was created with all light, all truth, all intelligence. And that is the truth, the whole truth, and nothing but the truth.

But the tribe of Reuben was divided;

they could not decide to come.

Why did they stay behind with the sheep?

To listen to shepherds calling the flocks?

Yes, the tribe of Reuben was divided;

they could not decide to come.

The tribe of Gad stayed east of the Jordan

and the tribe of Dan remained by the
ships

The tribe of Asher stayed by the sea-
coast. Instead they remained along the
shore.

*A word about the tribe of Dan. They
remained by the ships, which is exactly
what they were supposed to do. On the
journey of the Exodus, it was the tribe of
Dan who was given the responsibility of
serving as the rear guard, while Judah led
the Exodus under Moses and Aaron.*

*I have served in the armed forces—the
United States Marine Corps. In the armed
forces the rear guard is essential to the
battle, to protect the rear flank from
attack. If the enemy is aware that there is
no rear guard, what do you think they will
do? You are correct—the enemy will attack
the rear flank and inflict heavy casualties,
and the front troops will have to turn
around and go all the way back in order to
fight them. More than once this results in a
victorious battle for the enemy.*

*The tribes of Reuben and Gad, on the other
hand, protected the side flanks from attack
by the enemy. Let us never forget the
importance of all these military elements to*

the battle, otherwise there would be no victory to celebrate.

But the people of Zebulun and Naphtali

risked their lives on the battlefield.

I believe there is a bit of bragging going on here. It may be true that the tribes of Zebulun and Napthali risked their lives on the battlefield, but like I mentioned, without the other troops standing ready, or marching ready, whichever the case may be, there would be no victory.

So let me announce another eternal spiritual principle. I say spiritual because to God "all things are spiritual." He has stated before that "nothing I have created was not created spiritual first." If we think about this we can see it is true. How could God create a tree in the natural world if he had not already conceived it in his mind first.

So, first God created the tree in his mind, visualizing precisely what it would be like: the roots that absorb the nutrients of the soil and water, the water being drawn upward through the trunk and into the branches, and finally moving in and through the leaves.

The sunshine that shining down on the leaves, making them green, with the elements all combining to make the chlorophyll, and the leaves absorbing the carbon dioxide from the air and producing more growth—the carbon being a basic element for the growth of everything that exists. God creates all this in his mind (the spiritual) prior to creating the tree in the natural world.

<u>The glory of God is intelligence, or in other words, light and truth.</u>

At Taanach, by the stream of Megiddo,

the kings came and fought;

the kings of Canaan fought,

but they took no silver away.

The stars fought from the sky;

as they moved across the sky,

they fought against Sisera.

The chariots of Sisera were known to be at a distinct disadvantage after dark, when visibility was minimal.

A flood in the Kishon swept them away—by the on-rushing Kishon River.

The meaning here is twofold: first, the river made it difficult for the chariots to cross over to the other side, and second, the raging Kishon River delayed the forward movement of the commander's army.

I shall march, march on, with strength!

Then the horses came galloping on,

stamping the ground with their hoofs.

"Put a curse on Meroz," says the angel of

the Lord,

"a curse, a curse on those who live there.

They did not come to help the Lord,

come as soldiers to fight for him."

The most fortunate of women is Jael,

the wife of Heber the Kenite—

the most fortunate of women who live in tents.

Sisera asked for water, but she gave him milk;

she brought him cream in a beautiful bowl.

She took a tent peg in one hand,

a worker's hammer in the other;

she struck Sisera and crushed his skull;

she pierced him through the head.

He sank to his knees,

fell down and lay still at her feet.

At her feet he sank to his knees and fell;

he fell to the ground, dead.

Sisera, the failed commander of Jabin's great army, was given not respect by his host, because no respect was deserved. He was killed and died an ignominious death which he no doubt deserved. Disgraced in death as in life, his place in eternity is definitely suspect.

Sisera's mother looked out of the window;

she gazed from behind the lattice.

"Why is his chariot so late in coming?" she

asked.

 "Why are his horses so slow to return?"

Her wisest friends answered her,

and she told herself over and over,

"They are only finding things to capture

and divide,

a woman or two for every soldier,

rich cloth for Sisera,

embroidered pieces for the neck of the

queen."

And so goes the saying, "Only his mother could love him like that." Many times I have watched the parents of a young man who had committed a heinous and brutal crime, and I am always intrigued to hear the mother saying, "I never knew him like that. He was sometimes confused, yes, but all in all he was a good kid." Mothers love and care for their sons even when they don't deserve it, even when they become hardened criminals, even when they are locked up in the penitentiary for long periods of time, even when they are executed for the crime of murder. A mother cares for her son regardless of how he turns out. Mothers are created that way. That is how they look after and care for their sons. It is all part of God's perfect will for mothers. God loves us the same way, doesn't he? No matter what we may do or not do, God always will love us— unconditionally. Jesus didn't excuse his murderers. He did say, however, "Father forgive them, for they know not what they do."

One of the most important sayings of our Lord Jesus Christ was this: "Love your neighbor as you love me. This is the law (Love is the law). Forgive them and my Father will forgive you. Do not forgive them and the Father will not forgive you." (paraphrased from the Evangelist Matthew).

So may all your enemies die like that, O Lord,

but may your friends shine like the rising sun!

And there was peace in the land for forty years.

Deborah: Prophetess and Warrior

A New Commentary
by Gene Allen Groner

I would like to close this writing with a prayer for peace:

Our Father in heaven,

Thank you for the gift of your Holy Spirit, and for all the many gifts and blessings we receive from your gracious bounty. I am so grateful that you sent your Son Jesus to live among us, and to show us the way of love. Thank you for his life, and for his sacrifice on the cross for our salvation. I pray that everyone will come to receive Jesus Christ as the Lord and Savior of their life, and in so doing inherit the Kingdom of Heaven prepared by you from the very foundation of the world.

May our love and compassion for others increase day by day, and may we continue to grow in our faithfulness and in our witness of the Lord Jesus Christ. May your peace live in our hearts, in our homes, in our nation, and in the whole world, according to your perfect will.

In the precious name of your Son Jesus, the Savior of the World, I pray. Amen.

Biography

Gene Allen Groner is the Christian author of more than 35 inspirational books, plus numerous articles. He lives in Independence, Missouri with his wife of 54 years, a retired public health nurse. His interests include reading and writing, gardening, and volunteer work in the community. He is listed in Who's Who in Missouri, and is a lifetime member of the National Honor Society in Psychology, Psi Chi. Gene earned both the Bachelor and Master's Degrees with honors from Park University in Parkville, MO. He also attended the University of Hawaii and St. Paul School of Theology. He and his family are lifetime members of the Colonial Hills congregation in Blue Springs, MO.

geneallengroner@gmail.com

https://www.amazon.com/Gene-Allen-Groner/e/B077YTVSJZ

Notes

Notes

Printed by Amazon Italia Logistica S.r.l.
Torrazza Piemonte (TO), Italy

51891936R00029